Practical Science for Year 1

CW00683711

Introduction

This book of science activities aims to help the busy teacher deliver high quality science lessons with as much manageable practical classroom work as possible. This book is a major update of our previous Photocopiable Practical Science Series bringing it in line with the 2014 National Curriculum for England. Existing material has been rearranged and new material has been added making full curriculum coverage easy to complete.

For the latest catalogue:
Tel: 01772 863158
Fax: 01772 866153
e.mail: sales@topical-resources.co.uk
Buy online at:
www.topical-resources.co.uk

Topical Resources publishes a range of Educational Materials for use in Primary Schools and Pre-School Nurseries and Playgroups.

Topical Resources, P.O. Box 329, Broughton, Preston, Lancashire. PR3 5LT
Copyright © 2014 Viki Mason

Illustrated by John Hutchinson & Pat Lamb

Designed by Paul Sealey, PS3 Creative
3 Wentworth Drive, Thornton, Lancashire

Printed in the UK for 'Topical Resources' by T. Snape and Co Ltd, Boltons Court, Preston, Lancs.

First Published April 2014
ISBN: 978-1-909458-42-0

Topical Resources is the trading name of Topical Resources Ltd, registered in England number 8072582.

Registered office: Jumps Farm, Durton Lane, Broughton, Preston, Lancashire. PR3 5LE

Contents

Notes for Teachers

Health and Safety Guidance

This book has been written with reference to the Association for Science Education Publication 'Be Safe', ISBN 0 86357 324 X. It is intended that many of the activities described in this book should be carried out by children working independently in small groups. Every effort has been made to make sure that the activities are free from harm when carried out sensibly. However, it is understood that every classroom situation is different and consequently the final judgement of how the lessons are organised is up to the individual teacher. This should be done with reference to his/her own school health and safety policy. The author and the publisher can take no responsibility for any mishaps that occur during any practical science lesson.

Working Scientifically

'Working scientifically' is described separately at the beginning of the programme of study, but must always be taught through and clearly related to substantive science content in the programme of study.

Working Scientifically - Statutory requirements

During years 1 and 2, pupils should be taught to use the following practical scientific methods, processes and skills through the teaching of the programme of study content:

- asking simple questions and recognising that they can be answered in different ways
- observing closely, using simple equipment
- performing simple tests
- identifying and classifying
- using their observations and ideas to suggest answers to questions
- gathering and recording data to help in answering questions.

Notes and guidance (non-statutory)

Pupils in years 1 and 2 should explore the world around them and raise their own questions. They should experience different types of scientific enquiries, including practical activities, and begin to recognise ways in which they might answer scientific questions. They should use simple features to compare objects, materials and living things and, with help, decide how to sort and group them, observe changes over time, and, with guidance, they should begin to notice patterns and relationships. They should ask people questions and use simple secondary sources to find answers. They should use simple measurements and equipment (for example, hand lenses, egg timers) to gather data, carry out simple tests, record simple data, and talk about what they have found out and how they found it out. With help, they should record and communicate their findings in a range of ways and begin to use simple scientific language.

These opportunities for working scientifically should be provided across years 1 and 2 so that the expectations in the programme of study can be met by the end of year 2. Pupils are not expected to cover each aspect for every area of study.

Plants

Statutory requirements

Pupils should be taught to:
- identify and name a variety of common wild and garden plants, including deciduous and evergreen trees
- identify and describe the basic structure of a variety of common flowering plants, including trees.

Notes and guidance (non-statutory)

Pupils should use the local environment throughout the year to explore and answer questions about plants growing in their habitat. Where possible, they should observe the growth of flowers and vegetables that they have planted.

They should become familiar with common names of flowers, examples of deciduous and evergreen trees, and plant structures (including leaves, flowers (blossom), petals, fruit, roots, bulb, seed, trunk, branches, stem).

Pupils might work scientifically by: observing closely, perhaps using magnifying glasses, and comparing and contrasting familiar plants; describing how they were able to identify and group them, and drawing diagrams showing the parts of different plants including trees. Pupils might keep records of how plants have changed over time, for example the leaves falling off trees and buds opening; and compare and contrast what they have found out about different plants.

Lesson 1 – Be a Plant Detective!

Objective: To identify and name common wild and garden plants.
Resources: Page 6 photocopied for each child. You will need access to a variety of plants either in the school grounds or local area. A local nature walk would be preferable to see them in their natural environment.
Task: Tell the children about the area they are going to visit. Explain that they will carefully draw what they see, using magnifying glasses to help them. Ask questions during the walk such as: 'Why do you think this is growing here? 'Which plant is the tallest?' 'Which is the shortest?' 'Which plant is the most common here?' 'Which is your favourite?' Take photographs using digital cameras to capture what they have seen. Look at these when back inside.
Use the TALK ABOUT cards to promote discussion once back in the classroom.
Plan B: If it is difficult to access plants in the local environment, ask pupils to bring in plants from home. You may also like to ask staff members to bring in some plants to provide a greater variety and provide plants for children that have none at home.

Lesson 2 – Be a Tree Detective!

Objective: To identify and group deciduous and evergreen trees.
Resources: Page 8 photocopied for each child, prepared photos of a variety of trees if there are no opportunities to see them in the local area.
Task: Children will walk round the school grounds or local area looking at the different trees, making observations based on what they can see. They will draw pictures on their sheet and take photographs to capture what they have seen and to aid identification when back inside.
Use the TREE CARDS on page 9 to sort into two different groups.
NOTE: This task can be carried out at different times in the year to make comparisons and discuss changes including, which trees have lost their leaves and which are evergreen.

Lesson 3 – Two Plant Challenge

Objective: To identify and describe the structure of flowering plants.
Resources: Page 10 photocopied for each child, a selection of flowering plants with visible roots, magnifying glasses needed to look carefully at each part of the plant, library books or the internet for identification.
Task: Draw two flowering plants onto the sheet. Try to make sure that the plants are drawn above and below ground level. Use the magnifying glasses to look at the details. Colour in and name each plant; use the library books or search the internet to find out what they are called. Write their names on the sheet in the boxes.

Lesson 4 – Make a Tree Poster

Objective: To identify and describe the structure of trees.
Resources: Page 11 photocopied for each child, photographs, video clips or DVDs showing trees from around the country, binoculars if looking at trees nearby. Use library books or the internet as a resource. If necessary set a homework task for a few weeks before asking for families to go on a woodland walk or bring in some photographs to share with the class for this session.
Task: Children will create a poster or collage with the correct labels. They will cut out labels from the sheet and put them in the right place on their collage. Glue all the trees on to a large sheet of paper to display in school. It could be called 'Our Wonderful Woodland' display.

Lesson 5 – Through the Seasons

Objective: To observe and record changes over time through first hand practical experiences.
Resources: Enlarge pages 12, 13, 14 to A3 size and photocopy one for each child. Fold and cut along the dotted lines to create the diary. Add extra pages if necessary to include extra information e.g. photographs, scrapbook pictures, diagrams of trees and 'lift the flap' pages.
Task: Children will create their diary and add to it over the year to show changes through the seasons. It will need to include trees, plants and the local environment. Digital photographs and images could be included. Children could work in pairs or small groups or individually. Homework tasks could be set to add to the content of this exploration diary.

Lesson 6 (a) – Plant a Seed and Keep a Diary

Objective: To observe, record and present data on vegetable or flower growth over time.
Resources: Enlarge page 15 to A3 paper and photocopy one for each child. Fold along the dotted lines to make a diary. You will need seeds for planting, for example, broad bean seeds (that have been soaked overnight in water) and clear plastic named pots filled with compost. Rulers for measuring, magnifying glasses and digital cameras to record the growth and images of the flowers or the beans.
Task: Plant a seed and make sure that it can be seen. The children will need to keep it moist and in a warm place. They will observe their seeds over a period of weeks and record the growth and changes they can see. They can record any measurements and take photographs over time.

Lesson 6 (b) – Make a Block Graph

Objective: To gather and record simple data and talk about what they have found out and how they found it out. To record and communicate findings in a range of ways and begin to use simple scientific language.
Resources: Seeds and plastic pot as for page 15 and also tape measures with one copy of page 16 for each child.
Task: Children will complete the block graph individually or work in pairs to show the growth of the plant in cm over time.

Lesson 7 – Plan a TV Plant Programme

Objective: To become familiar with, and use correctly, common names of flowers, trees and plant structures. To begin to use simple scientific language to talk about what they have found and communicate their ideas to a range of audiences, in a variety of ways.
Resources: Clips taken from TV wildlife programmes and Children's Television shows, digital camera recorders, digital cameras to take still photographs, page 17 photocopied for each group or pair to plan their ideas.
Task: The children will work together to plan their own TV programme about the local area; trees and plants; changes; and any interesting facts they have found out through this topic of work. Children must use the keywords provided on the sheet within their TV plan. Practise the TV programme together and then each one can be filmed and watched together as a class at the end of the topic.

Be a Plant Detective!

Name:_____ Date:_____

Plant Name:

Plant Name:

Plant Name:

Plant Name:

Plant Name:

Plant Name:

Draw a different plant on each petal and write their names.

Talk About Plants

My plant is as tall as ...

My plant is as small as ...

My plant is the same as ...

My plant is different because...

My plant is as soft as ...

My plant is usually found ...

My plant is like ...

My plant is ...

Be a Tree Detective!

Name:_____ Date: _____

Draw some trees in the boxes.

Evergreen trees
keep leaves in winter.

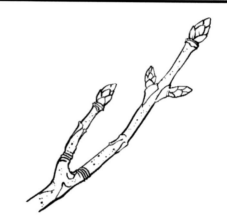

Deciduous trees
lose leaves in winter.

Tree Cards

 Can you sort these trees into two different groups?

Sycamore

Oak

Willow

Horse Chestnut

Beech

Ash

Giant Redwood

Giant Sequoia

Douglas Fir

Western Red Cedar

European Larch

Italian Cypress

Two Plant Challenge

Name:_____ Date: _____

Carefully draw two different flowering plants. Use these words to label them.

| flower | petal | stem | root | leaf |

Above ground

Below ground

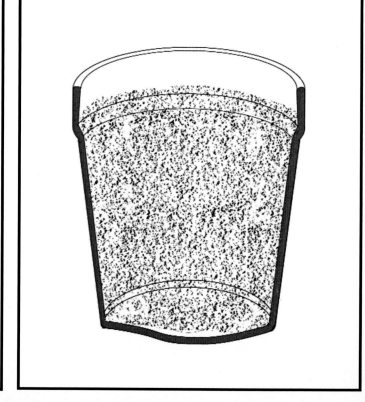

Make a Tree Poster

Name:_____   Date: _____

Decorate the tree shape. Stick the labels in the correct places.

| roots | trunk | leaves | branch | twig |

Trees Through the Seasons

Cut along the solid lines. Fold the dotted lines to make a 'Tree Diary'.

Autumn Trees by _____

Summer Trees by _____

Winter Trees by _____

Spring Trees by _____

Flowering Plants
Through the Seasons

Cut along the solid lines. Fold the dotted lines to make a 'Flowering Plants Diary'.

Autumn Flowering Plants by _____

Summer Flowering Plants by _____

Winter Flowering Plants by _____

Spring Flowering Plants by _____

'Local Views' Through the Seasons

Cut along the solid lines. Fold the dotted lines to make a 'Local Views Diary'.

Autumn Views by _____

Summer Views by _____

Winter Views by _____

Spring Views by _____

Plant a Seed and Keep a Diary

Cut along the solid lines. Fold the dotted line to make a 'Seed Diary'.

A Diary of a Seed by

Week 5

Week 1

Week 4

Week 2

Week 3

Make a Block Graph

Name:_____ Date: _____

Colour the squares to show how high your plant is at the end of each week.

Height of Plant

	Week 1	Week 2	Week 3	Week 4
20cm				
18cm				
16cm				
14cm				
12cm				
10cm				
8cm				
6cm				
4cm				
2cm				
0cm				

Plan a TV Plant Programme

Name:_____   Date: _____

Take some digital pictures. Plan what you will say about each one. Get someone to film you. Use these words.

leaves	flowers	stem	roots
branches	fruit	trunk	twigs

1 Picture

Script:

_____

_____

_____

_____

2 Picture

Script:

_____

_____

_____

_____

3 Picture

Script:

_____

_____

_____

_____

4 Picture

Script:

_____

_____

_____

_____

Animals, including Humans

Statutory requirements

Pupils should be taught to:
- identify and name a variety of common animals including fish, amphibians, reptiles, birds and mammals
- identify and name a variety of common animals that are carnivores, herbivores and omnivores
- describe and compare the structure of a variety of common animals (fish, amphibians, reptiles, birds and mammals, including pets)
- identify, name, draw and label the basic parts of the human body and say which part of the body is associated with each sense.

Notes and guidance (non-statutory)

Pupils should use the local environment throughout the year to explore and answer questions about animals in their habitat. They should understand how to take care of animals taken from their local environment and the need to return them safely after study. Pupils should become familiar with the common names of some fish, amphibians, reptiles, birds and mammals, including those that are kept as pets.

Pupils should have plenty of opportunities to learn the names of the main body parts (including head, neck, arms, elbows, legs, knees, face, ears, eyes, hair, mouth, teeth) through games, actions, songs and rhymes.

Pupils might work scientifically by: using their observations to compare and contrast animals at first hand or through videos and photographs, describing how they identify and group them; grouping animals according to what they eat; and using their senses to compare different textures, sounds and smells.

Lesson 1 – Who Am I?

Objective: To identify and name common animals.
Resources: Page 22 photocopied for each pair or small group. Enlarge to A3 if necessary.
Task: Children will cut out and match the different cards together. They can use the blank cards at the bottom of the sheet to make their own, if able to. Using mixed ability pairs or groups will enable all the children to work together and help each other with this task. Encourage the groups to share their ideas and talk about what they already know.

Lesson 2 – What do I Like To Eat?

Objective: To identify, group and classify animals according to what they like to eat.
Resources: Page 23 photocopied for each child, animal cards cut out ready to use if necessary, TV clips showing different animals from around the world eating their food. The Internet will provide plenty of photographs and other resources to help with this task.
Task: The children can match the animal cards to the right places in the Venn diagram.

Lesson 3 – What do I Look Like?

Objective: To label and talk about the features of different animals.
Resources: Page 24 photocopied for each child to use, library books with detailed photographs or pictures showing animals in more detail.
Task: The children will look at the pictures at the top of the sheet to help them identify the different features of each animal. They then tick off which features they have, identifying what kind of animal it is in the end column.

Lesson 4 – What do Pets Eat and Drink?

Objective: To understand how to take care of pets and talk about how they are similar or different.
Resources: Page 25 photocopied for each child, a variety of real pets brought in by other staff and/or children during the week. For example, have a 'Pet Week' in school and invite an adult in with each pet, to talk about how they look after them. If this is not possible then you will need a good selection of library books and film clips or DVDs.
Task: Children will complete the grid based on what they have seen and understood.

Lesson 5 – Amazing Animal Facts

Objective: To compare and contrast animals and talk about how you can group them. To create an identification 'top trumps' set of cards for animals you know.
Resources: Pages 26 and 27 photocopied for each child, library books and other resources where children can find their facts. Size could be small, medium or large decided after class discussion.
Task: The children will work together in small groups or pairs to make their own Top Trumps cards to share in the classroom. Once completed the children can see which animals 'win' each category, where appropriate. Encourage discussion around each card. Teach the children how to play the Top Trumps game.

Lesson 6 – The Sense of Touch / Smell

Objective: To use senses to compare different textures and smells.
Resources: Page 28 photocopied for each child. Prepare some 'texture trays' or boxes before the session. Include a selection of the following items inside the boxes or on top of each tray: cotton wool, string, plasticine or play dough, plastic straw, gravel, tissue paper, tin foil, rubber bands, crumbly cheese, cold baked beans, jelly, sandpaper and corrugated cardboard. The 'smell bottle' (or other containers) could include egg, rose petals, perfume, banana, lemon, talcum powder, coffee, onion, herbs e.g. rosemary and mint, spices e.g. ginger.
Task: Ask the children to work in small groups to touch or smell the different items. They must then record their thoughts and comments on the sheet provided. They could go round each tray or bottle with a partner or arrange them in groups to carry out the activity.

Lesson 7 – Body Parts

Objective: To identify, name and label the basic parts of the human body.
Resources: Page 30 photocopied for each child. Library books or Internet resources with photographs and labels about body parts for the children to use.
Task: Play 'Simon Says' or sing 'Heads, Shoulders, Knees and Toes' at the start of the activity. The children must first make their play dough or plasticine model of themselves; see picture provided on the sheet. They will then talk together as a group and help each other to complete a collage or large poster either in pairs or individually to show a labelled diagram of body parts. (including head, neck, arms, elbows, legs, knees, face, ears, eyes, hair, mouth, teeth). Encourage good discussion about what the body parts do and how they help them to carry out everyday tasks.

Lesson 8 – Plan and Carry Out an Investigation

Objective: To work scientifically to find out about animals in the local area.
Resources: Page 31, 32, 33, 34 (depending on ability) photocopied for each child or small group. Resources needed will vary depending upon the investigation chosen.
Task (1): The children could research and set up a bird hide in the school grounds or a digital camera set up with a bird feeding table or bird bath. Different foods such as nuts, seeds, balls of fat etc. could be placed outside daily and time allowed for volunteers to observe at regular intervals. This could be two or three children each time slot. A tally sheet could be used to record which are the most popular of the foods on offer.
Task (2): Plan a trip around the local area or to a local farm/park. Local countryside rangers can often help with this kind of activity. An animal count could be made over a period of time either in the school garden e.g. rabbit or squirrel watch. The children will record what they see including the different types of animals. Feeding habits could also be observed over time.

Lesson 9 – Be a Sense Detective

Objective: To work scientifically to find out about our senses.
Resources: Page 35 photocopied for each child or small group to complete. A selection of resources to include rulers, tape measures, stop watches, magnifying glasses and timers. The list of sense station items is provided below.
Task: The children must spend time at each 'sense station'. They will be 'detectives' and investigate the clues at each station using the boxes provided. Examples of items provided at each station are:
- Taste: salt, strawberry, lemon, sugar, cheese, red pepper
- Touch: sandpaper, cotton ball, bean bag, ice, rock, sand
- Smell: liquorice, old shoe, fragrant flower, orange, cinnamon
- Hearing: bell, wind chime, drumstick, ticking clock, water-filled container, tin filled with rice
- Sight: watercolours, fabrics, bowl, old telephone, stuffed animal, shoe.

Who Am I?

Cut out, mix up and match the shapes.
Talk about each animal.

I have fur.
My young are
called puppies.
I have 4 legs.

I can see at
night. I can
fly. I have a
sharp beak.

I have a fin.
I have a snout.
I swim very
fast.

I lay eggs in
water.
I can swim.
I can hop.

I eat shell fish.
I have big eyes.
I have 8 long
arms.

I have antlers.
I can run fast.
I eat grass.

My shell is hard.
I eat algae. I
have sharp
claws.

I live on a
farm.
I like mud.
I am very fat.

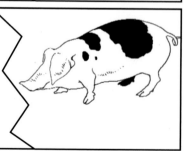

I live in the sea.
I have five
points. My
body is spiky.

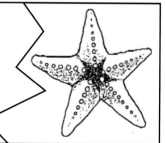

I live on a
farm.
I eat grass.
I make milk.

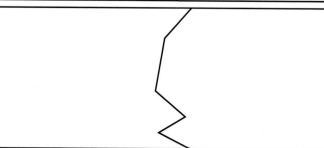

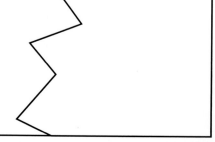

What do I Like to Eat?

Name:_____   Date: _____

Cut out the animals and stick them on the chart to show what they like to eat.

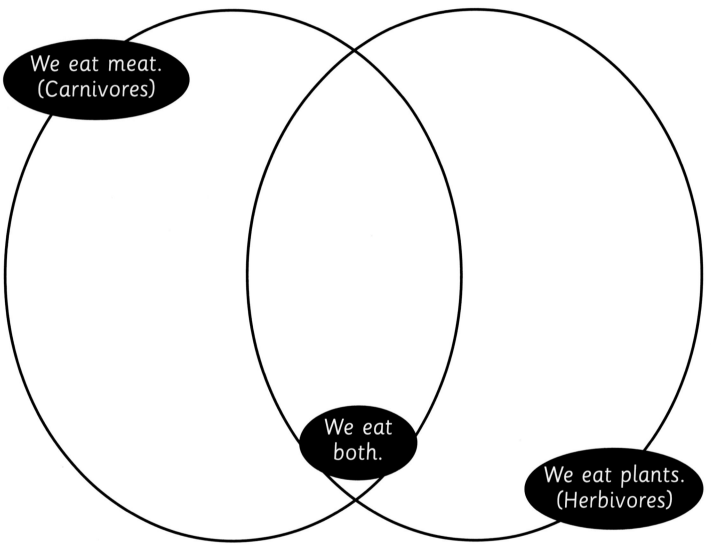

We eat meat. (Carnivores)

We eat both.

We eat plants. (Herbivores)

What do I Look Like?

Name: _____ Date: _____

Look at the pictures and talk about the different types of animal. Then tick or cross each box below.

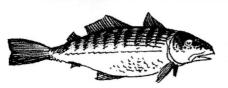

Fish
- breathes with gills
- lives in water
- has scaly skin

Bird
- has wings
- has a beak
- has feathers

Amphibian
- lives on land and in water
- has cold blood

Mammal
- has fur
- feeds young with milk
- has warm blood

Reptile
- lays eggs
- has scaly skin
- has cold blood

Tick or cross each box.

	gills	scales	beak	whiskers	claws	tail	fur	hooves	paws	wings	I am a?

What do Pets Eat and Drink?

Name:_____   Date:_____

All animals need different things. Record what you find out from your group on the chart below.

Pet	Food	Likes	Dislikes	Needs

Why do animals need food and drink?

_____

_____

Amazing Animal Facts

Cut out the cards. Get help to find out the missing facts. Learn how to play 'Top Trumps'.

Snake	Frog	Dove	Tiger
Size _____	Size _____	Size _____	Size _____
Life Span _____	Life Span _____	Life Span _____	Life Span _____

Lion	Monkey	Newt	Bat
Size _____	Size _____	Size _____	Size _____
Life Span _____	Life Span _____	Life Span _____	Life Span _____

Worm	Crocodile	Bee	Butterfly
Size _____	Size _____	Size _____	Size _____
Life Span _____	Life Span _____	Life Span _____	Life Span _____

Amazing Animal Facts

Cut out the cards. Get help to find out the missing facts. Learn how to play 'Top Trumps'.

Bear	Spider	Gorilla	Dog

Size _____ Size _____ Size _____ Size _____

Life Span _____ Life Span _____ Life Span _____ Life Span _____

Cat	Crab	Rabbit	Chick

Size _____ Size _____ Size _____ Size _____

Life Span _____ Life Span _____ Life Span _____ Life Span _____

Salmon	Pig	Horse	Camel

Size _____ Size _____ Size _____ Size _____

Life Span _____ Life Span _____ Life Span _____ Life Span _____

The Sense of Touch

Name:_____ Date: _____

Touch different materials.
What do they feel like?

What I touched	What it felt like
elastic band	
sandpaper	

The Sense of Smell

Name: _____ Date: _____

Smell different objects.
What do they smell like?

What I smelled	What it smelt like
perfume	
banana	

Body Parts

Name:_____ Date:_____

Make a model of yourself and talk about it.

Now make a large picture of a boy or a girl. Use the labels below on your picture.

 head	 body	

head

eyes

nose

ears

mouth

teeth

body

leg

hands

feet

knee

arm

Plan and Carry Out a Birdwatching Investigation

Name:_____ Date: _____

My question is... What do birds like to eat?

Equipment List

bird table
water bowl
bag of nuts
ball of fat
seeds

Method

I will change

I will keep this the same

I will measure and record

This is how I will make my test fair

I predict that:

Some useful words:
blue tit, robin, finch, sparrow, hide

Plan and Carry Out a Birdwatching Investigation

Name:_____ Date: _____

My question is...
What do birds like to eat?

What I will need:

What I will do:

I predict that:

Word Bank: bird table, water bowl, nuts, fat, seeds, blue tit, robin, sparrow, finch, hide

Plan and Carry Out a Wildlife Investigation

Name:_____ Date: _____

My question is... Which is the best place for wildlife?

Equipment List

clipboard
paper
pencil

Method

I will change

The places I go.

I will keep this the same

How long I spend at each location.

I will measure and record

This is how I will make my test fair

I predict that:

Some useful words:
study, observe, count, watch

Plan and Carry Out
a Wildlife Investigation

Name:_____ Date: _____

My question is...
Which is the best place for wildlife?

What I will need:

What I will do:

I predict that:

Word Bank:
study, observe, count, watch

Be a Sense Detective

Name:_____ Date: _____

I like the smell of...

_____

I don't like the smell of...

_____

I like the feel of...

_____

I don't like the feel of...

_____

I like the taste of...

_____

I don't like the taste of...

_____

I like to listen to...

_____

I don't like to listen to...

_____

Me

I like to look at...

_____

I don't like to look at...

_____

Everyday Materials

Statutory requirements

Pupils should be taught to:
- distinguish between an object and the material from which it is made
- identify and name a variety of everyday materials, including wood, plastic, glass, metal, water, and rock
- describe the simple physical properties of a variety of everyday materials
- compare and group together a variety of everyday materials on the basis of their simple physical properties.

Notes and guidance (non-statutory)

Pupils should explore, name, discuss and raise and answer questions about everyday materials so that they become familiar with the names of materials and properties such as: hard/soft; stretchy/stiff; shiny/dull; rough/smooth; bendy/not bendy; waterproof/not waterproof; absorbent/not absorbent; opaque/transparent. Pupils should explore and experiment with a wide variety of materials, not only those listed in the programme of study, but including for example: brick, paper, fabrics, elastic, foil.

Pupils might work scientifically by: performing simple tests to explore questions, for example: 'What is the best material for an umbrella? ...for lining a dog basket? ...for curtains? ...for a bookshelf? ...for a gymnast's leotard?'

Lesson 1 – Material Hunt Around the Room

Objective: To distinguish between an object and the material from which it is made.
Resources: Page 40 photocopied for each child, clip boards – one per child, pencils.
Task: The children will work individually to find different objects around the classroom or school. They will then complete the sheet to show what materials they are made out of. Ensure that there is a range within the area, for example, rolling the blind down a little way so that they can feel it. Ensure that the radiator is not too hot to the touch.

Lesson 2 – Talk About Materials

Objective: To identify and name everyday materials. To raise and answer questions about everyday materials.
Resources: Page 41 photocopied for each child and page 42 photocopied for each group.
Task: Children will each have one sheet containing the drawings of different objects and they will ask and answer questions in their group about the objects on their sheet. They must take turns and each say something. Then at the end they must ask their own questions using the six prompt cards at the bottom of the sheet.

Lesson 3 – What If…? Questions

Objective: To understand that there are many different materials that can be named and described. To understand that materials can be used in a variety of ways.
Resources: Page 43 photocopied for each child, blank plain A4 paper for each child to draw a picture on.
Task: Each child will read and answer the 'What if…?' questions on the sheet. Then they must choose one question to draw in more detail, explaining the consequences of the 'What if…?' challenge. For example the drawings for the 'What if chairs were made of chocolate' might show someone squashing a chair by sitting on it or someone eating a chair.

Lesson 4 – Plan a Perfect Bedroom

Objective: To use knowledge about different everyday objects and the materials they are made from to design an ideal bedroom, with labels.
Resources: Page 44 photocopied for each child, various home-style magazines and shopping catalogues or brochures collected from the class and other school staff. Use the images to help them with ideas.
Task: The children will work in pairs to help each other plan their own bedroom design. They should include the labels on the sheet and use the template given to complete the activity. The different materials must be thought about carefully.

Lesson 5 – Plan and carry out a Waterproof Fabric Investigation

Objective: To perform a simple test for different materials to see how waterproof they are. To communicate what they did, what happened, making simple comparisons and recording results.
Resources: Page 45 or page 46 photocopied one per child, various materials for testing including; nylon, wool, cotton, silk, lycra, denim and leather.
Task: The children will work in small groups to carry out simple investigations based on waterproofing. They will use one of the sheets to record their ideas. They can work in mixed ability groups to enable all the children to participate.

Lesson 6 – Make a Material Collage

Objective: To create a wall display / scrapbook / poster to show comparisons between a variety of everyday materials.
Resources: Page 47 photocopied for each group or pair, samples and scrap pieces of various materials for their collage or scrapbook work. For example: ball of wool, string, cotton wool, cloths, felt shapes, tissue paper, cardboard, tin foil, coloured plastic wallets cut up, paper, card, old jeans cut up etc.
Task: The groups or pairs will work together to create a bright, colourful poster or scrapbook for display in the classroom or on the corridor. They will explore a range of materials and then demonstrate the features of each one, labelling any differences or similarities. Digital photographs could also be used as part of the display which can also include outside materials from around the school grounds or local area.

Lesson 7 – What Am I?

Objective: To know that materials have different physical properties. To suggest uses for different materials.
Resources: Page 48 photocopied for each group. The teacher needs to prepare simple 'ring hats', one for each child. It may be necessary to enlarge this resource sheet to A3 size.
Task: Each child will work with a partner or in a small group to play this game. Each child is given a hat to wear without them seeing the image on the front. The children take it in turns to ask a question about their own hat and are given the answer yes or no. The winner is the one who guesses their own material first. They can go round the group and take turns to ensure that it is fair.

Lesson 8 – Test to See if... True Or False?

Objective: To describe the simple physical properties of a variety of everyday objects through a true/ false activity.
Resources: Page 49 photocopied for each child. All the items identified on the grid to include: chocolate pieces, paper, Lego brick and small tub of water, balls of wool, cardboard box pieces, play dough, some stones, elastic bands, clay pieces.
Task: Each child will work on different activities, which will be set up around the room. They will carry out each task as explained on the sheet and then record the result and move on, using observation skills to record what happened and whether it was a true or false statement each time. Encourage plenty of predictions before each test.

Lesson 9 – Plan and Carry Out a Floating and Sinking Investigation

Objective: To test various materials to see which ones float or sink over time. To record and talk about their findings from the investigation.
Resources: Use pages 52 and 53 photocopied for each child to record the results of the investigation. Various items to test include: stones, table tennis balls, sponges, plasticine, toy cars, ball of newspaper, boat shaped paper, tin foil ball, tin foil boat, pencil, paper plate, plastic straw, chalk etc. Use timers to time the test.
Task: Discuss Page 50 or page 51 depending on ability of group to plan the investigation. The children will complete the sheet to explain what they have done. They will carry out each investigation and use a timer to ensure that they are carrying out a fair test. They could also use digital cameras to record each outcome and then create a display with labels.

Material Hunt Around the Room

Name:_____   Date: _____

 Look around your classroom for different materials. Tick the boxes in the chart below.

Materials / Objects	glass	plastic	wood	fabric	paper	metal
window						
computer						
cupboard						
floor						
desk						
chair						
blinds						
door						
radiator						
books						

Talk About Materials

Name:_____ Date:_____

Can you answer questions about these objects?

brick	stone	ball of string	elastic band
pencil	ruler	play dough	sponge
ball	Lego brick	scissors	paper clip
Blu-tac	spoon	wood	cotton reel

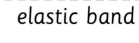

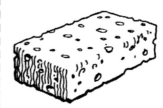

Question Cards

What would you use this for?

What is this made from?

How do you think this is made?

What is this called?

Where would this object be used?

How old do you think this is?

Can you get this in different sizes?

Who might use this object?

What...?

Why...?

Where...?

How...?

Who...?

When...?

What if...? Questions

Name:_____ Date: _____

Talk about these questions.
Write what would happen.

1. What if 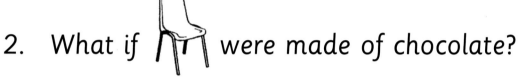 were made of Blu-tac?

----

2. What if were made of chocolate?

----

3. What if  were made of paper?

----

4. What if were made of string?

----

5. What if  were made of wood?

Draw a picture of one of these mistakes.
Remember to add some labels.

Plan a Perfect Bedroom

Name:_____ Date: _____

Draw your perfect bedroom. Include a bed, desk, chair, wardrobe, windows, door and some choices of your own.

Cut out the material words and label your drawing.

| wood | glass | cotton | plastic | paper | metal |

Plan and Carry Out a Waterproof Fabric Investigation

Name: _____ Date: _____

My question is...
Which fabrics will keep me dry?

What I will need:

What I will do:

I predict that:

Word Bank
nylon, wool, cotton, silk, lycra, denim and leather

Plan and Carry Out a Waterproof Fabric Investigation

Name:_____ Date: _____

My question is...
Which fabrics will keep me dry?

Equipment List

Method

I will change

I will keep this the same

The size of each piece of fabric.

The amount of water dropped on the fabric.

I will measure and record

If the fabric...
keeps out water
or
lets water through
or
soaks water up.

This is how I will make my test fair

I predict that:

You will need nylon, wool, cotton, silk, lycra, denim and leather.

Make a Material Collage

Stick these words to a large sheet of paper then find material examples to display next to each word.

bendy	stiff	hard	soft
stretchy	squashy	shiny	dull
absorbent	not absorbent	opaque (not see-through)	transparent (see-through)
rough	smooth	waterproof	not waterproof

What Am I?

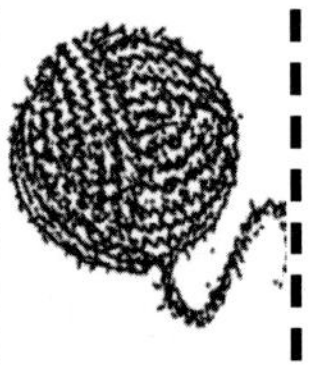

wool

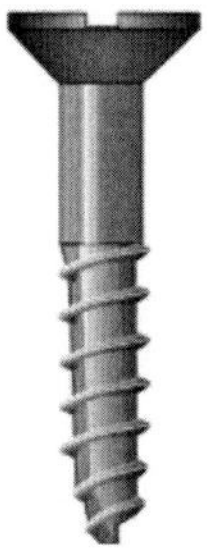

metal

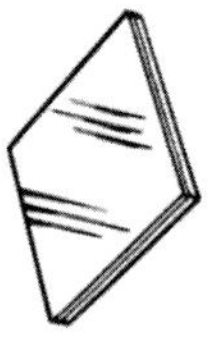

glass

paper

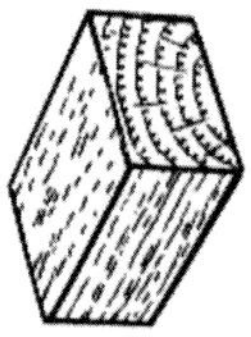

wood

cotton

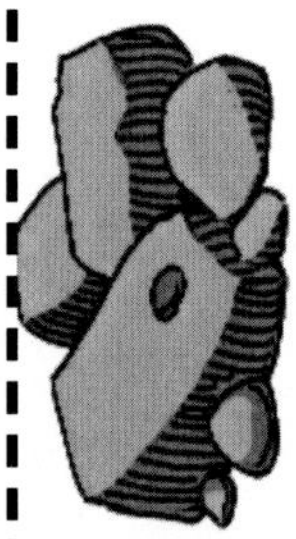

stone

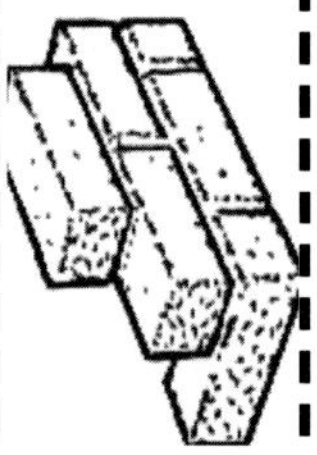

brick

cardboard

Test to see if... True or False?

Name:_____ Date: _____

Take turns to test each statement and then put a tick in either the true or false box.

		True	False
1	A piece of clay can bounce.		
2	An elastic band can stretch.		
3	A stone can twist and bend.		
4	A Lego brick can stretch.		
5	A chocolate bar can bend.		
6	A ball of wool can bounce.		
7	A toy car will float better than a piece of card.		
8	Play dough will sink.		
9	A wet piece of card will sink.		
10	A dry piece of paper will float.		

Can you make a ball of plasticine float?

_____

Plan and Carry Out a Floating and Sinking Investigation

Name:_____   Date: _____

My question is...
Which materials float?

What I will need:

What I will do:

I predict that:

Word Bank

float, shape, water, place, sink, heavy, light, drop

Plan and Carry Out a Floating and Sinking Investigation

Name:_____ Date: _____

My question is...
Which materials float?

Equipment List

Method

I will change

I will keep this the same

How each material is placed in the bowl.
The same amount of water in the bowl

I will measure and record

Which materials float?

Which materials sink?

This is how I will make my test fair

I predict that:

Some useful words:
float, water, shape, place, sink, heavy, light, drop.

Which Materials Float?

Name:_____ Date:_____

Tick which you think will float or sink.
Test to see if your prediction was correct.

Object		Float	Sink	Correct? Yes or No
coin				
peg				
plastic duck				
scissors				
crayon				
paper clip				
toy car				
stamp				
pencil				
Lego brick				
rubber				

Which Materials Float?

Name:_____ Date: _____

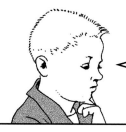

Tick which you think will float or sink.
Test to see if your prediction was correct.

Object	Float	Sink	Correct? Yes or No
stone			
plastic ball			
sponge			
plasticine			
newspaper (ball)			
paper boat			
tin foil ball			
tin foil boat			
paper plate			
plastic straw			
chalk			

Year 1 Programme of Study

Seasonal Changes

Statutory requirements

Pupils should be taught to:
- observe changes across the four seasons
- observe and describe weather associated with the seasons and how day length varies.

Notes and guidance (non-statutory)

Pupils should observe and talk about changes in the weather and the seasons.
Note: Pupils should be warned that it is not safe to look directly at the Sun, even when wearing dark glasses.
Pupils might work scientifically by: making tables and charts about the weather; and making displays of what happens in the world around them, including day length, as the seasons change.

Lesson 1 – Sing a Song of Seasons

Objective: To know and understand the different features of each season and relate this to real life situations.
Resources: One copy of the song sheet for each child (also consider sending a copy home for homework), coloured pens and pencils to decorate a border.
Task: Sing the song to the class to the tune of 'Twinkle Twinkle, Little Star'. Help them to create their own actions to help them learn each verse. Add instruments if possible and record the song to use throughout the year when returning to this topic of seasonal changes.

Make a Seasonal Year Diary

Objective: An A4 or A3 seasonal scrapbook for each child.
Resources: Photocopies of all the activity sheets for this topic, one per child, various photographs sourced from the Internet or collected through homework activities and other classes, other school staff.
Task: The children will work on their own diaries using A4 or A3 scrapbooks (dependent on classroom storage facilities). They could supply their own if necessary and personalise the front cover. All the tasks carried out over the year through this unit of study will make up the diary. Additional homework tasks could also be used to enable children to monitor changes in their own gardens or parks and playgrounds. Photographs of changes will also be included through school and home based activities. Any sketches created by the children, using magnifying glasses would also enhance this diary.

Autumn Days
Lesson 2 - Record One Week of Autumn Weather
Objective: To observe and talk about changes in the weather: focus on wind/rain.

Lesson 3 - Take a Walk and Record 'Signs of Autumn'
Objective: To observe and describe signs of Autumn.

Lesson 4 - Autumn Leaves
Objective: To identify different trees by their leaves in Autumn.

Winter Days
Lesson 5 - Record One Week of Winter Weather
Objective: To observe and talk about changes in the weather: focus on temperature/cloud.

Lesson 6 - Take a Walk and Record 'Signs of Winter'
Objective: To observe and describe signs of Winter.

Lesson 7 - Winter Twigs
Objective: To identify different trees by their twigs in Winter.

Spring Days
Lesson 8 - Record One Week of Spring Weather
Objective: To observe and describe changes in the weather: focus on sunshine/rain.

Lesson 9 - Take a Walk and Record 'Signs of Spring'
Objective: To observe and describe signs of Spring.

Lesson 10 - Photograph 'New Growth' in Spring
Objective: To collect evidence of new growth using a digital camera.

Summer Days
Lesson 11 - Record One Week of Summer Weather
Objective: To observe and describe changes in the weather: focus on sunshine/ temperature.

Lesson 12 - Take a Walk and Record 'Signs of Summer'
Objective: To observe and describe signs of Summer.

Lesson 13 - Flowers Bloom in Summer
Objective: To photograph / sketch flowers seen.

Sing a Song of Seasons

Name:_____ Date: _____

Sing this song to the tune of 'Twinkle Twinkle, Little Star', then decorate the border.

1) Spring time, Spring time, here you are.
   Plants grow, lambs jump, baa baa baa!
   Spring time showers; splash and play.
   Daffodils, tulips. Sunny day!
   Spring time, Spring time, grass is green.
   It is such a beautiful scene.

2) Summer time, Summer time, lots of fun.
   Beach trips, sandcastles in the sun!
   Summer time heat, ice-creams we eat.
   Fruit and berries what a treat!
   Summer time, Summer time, we love you.
   We can't wait to barbeque.

3) Autumn time, Autumn time, leaves will fall.
   Winds blow, longer nights for all!
   Autumn time conkers, acorns too.
   Dark skies, bonfire, fireworks – Wahoo!
   Autumn time, Autumn time, crunch, crunch, crunch.
   Toffee apples, munch, munch, munch.

4) Winter time, Winter time, here comes snow.
   Sledging and sliding, here we go!
   Winter time frosts, wrap up warm.
   Hats, gloves, scarves protect from a storm!
   Winter time, Winter time, twinkly lights.
   It is such a beautiful sight.

Record One Week of Autumn Weather

Name:_____ Date: _____

	🌧	☀	🪁	☁	🌡	hours of daylight
Monday						
Tuesday						
Wednesday						
Thursday						
Friday						
Saturday						
Sunday						

Take a Walk and Record
'Signs of Autumn'

Name:_____ Date: _____

My Autumn Picture

Autumn Leaves

Name:_____ Date:_____

Some leaves change colour in autumn.
Colour these drawings in autumn shades.

Oak

Ash

Horse Chestnut

Beech

Hawthorn

Sycamore

Record One Week of Winter Weather

Name:_____ Date: _____

						hours of daylight
Monday						
Tuesday						
Wednesday						
Thursday						
Friday						
Saturday						
Sunday						

Take a Walk and Record 'Signs of Winter'

Name:_____ Date:_____

My Winter Picture

Winter Twigs

Name:_____ Date: _____

Some winter twigs have buds where new leaves will grow. Collect and sketch winter twigs like those shown below.

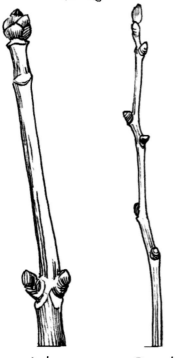

Ash   Beech   Horse Chestnut   Oak   Hawthorn   Sycamore

My Winter Twigs

Record One Week of Spring Weather

Name:_____ Date:_____

	☔	☀	🪁	☁	🌡	hours of daylight
Monday						
Tuesday						
Wednesday						
Thursday						
Friday						
Saturday						
Sunday						

Take a Walk and Record 'Signs of Spring'

Name:_____ Date: _____

   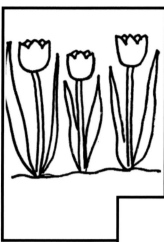

My Spring Picture

Photograph 'New Growth' in Spring

Name:_____ Date:_____

In Spring new shoots begin to grow and blossom appears on trees. Use a digital camera to record 'new growth.

Image 1

Image 2

Image 3

Image 4

Image 5

Image 6

Record One Week of Summer Weather

Name:_____ Date:_____

						hours of daylight
Monday						
Tuesday						
Wednesday						
Thursday						
Friday						
Saturday						
Sunday						

Take a Walk and Record 'Signs of Summer'

Name:_____ Date:_____

My Summer Picture